Contents

G000139708

About this book

Most of the work in this book is for you to do on your own.

Sometimes you will work with a friend.

You will need instructions from your teacher to do some of the work.

Sometimes you need things to help you. The pictures at the bottom of each page show you what you need.

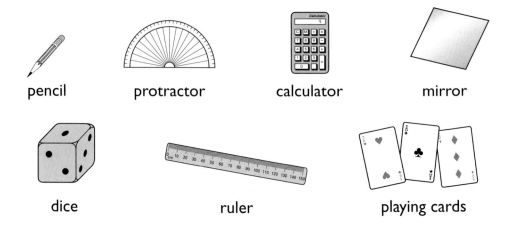

pencil   protractor   calculator   mirror

dice   ruler   playing cards

At the bottom of some pages, there is extra work your teacher might ask you to do. It has a key next to it, like this:

Work carefully! Read each question all the way through before trying to work out the answer.

Do not write in this book.

Ordering numbers

Which bird in each pair has flown further?

Copy each pair of distances and write $<$ or $>$ between them.

Work out the difference.

1.

13 345 km   14 543 km

2.

24 600 km   23 090 km

3.

10 616 km   9 999 km

4.

11 710 km   17 107 km

5. John's car cost between £7000 and £8251. Write five possible prices in words and digits.

6. Write these numbers in descending order.

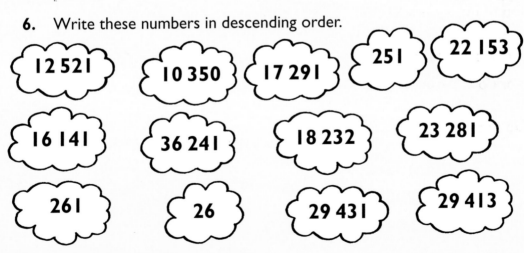

12 521   10 350   17 291   251   22 153

16 141   36 241   18 232   23 281

261   26   29 431   29 413

7. Write each number in words.

Write a number which is between 50 and 100 more than each number. Use words and digits.

1

Negative numbers

1. Write the number to which each hand is pointing.

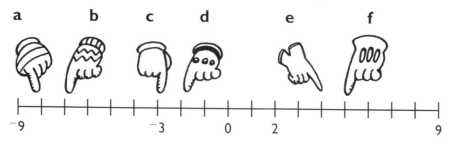

2. The thermometer shows the temperature in Jake's garden pond.

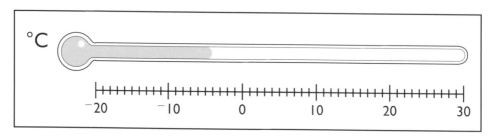

Write the temperature.

3. He pours in some hot water and the temperature rises by 5 °C.

What is the new temperature?

4. During the day, the temperature in the pond drops by 8 °C. Now what is the temperature?

5. In the night, the temperature drops again to ⁻11 °C. How much did it drop?

6. Write the difference between each pair of temperatures:

5 °C and 15 °C

3 °C and 10 °C

⁻2 °C and 4 °C

⁻4 ° C and 0 °C

At night the temperature in the pond is below freezing but above ⁻20°C.
The maximum temperature is 8°C higher than the minimum temperature.
Write some possible maximum and minimum temperatures.

Problems

Write how many birds on each roof.

1.

6 birds on each chimney
15 chimneys

2.

7 birds on each chimney
23 chimneys

3.

9 birds on each chimney
14 chimneys

4.

8 birds on each chimney
11 chimneys

5.

5 birds on each chimney
13 chimneys

6.

6 birds on each chimney
16 chimneys

How many boxes are needed?

7. 27 pears

3 to a box

8. 42 tomatoes

6 to a box

9. 45 plums

9 to a box

10. 32 peaches

8 to a box

Look at the fruit numbers. Write all the numbers that are a multiple of:

11. 3   **12.** 2   **13.** 4   **14.** 5

15. 6   **16.** 9   **17.** 8   **18.** 7

 49

72

 100

54

64

 70

42

 56

99

81

 66

 24

48

45

Special offer

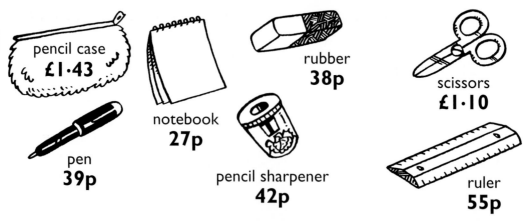

pencil case
£1·43

notebook
27p

rubber
38p

scissors
£1·10

pen
39p

pencil sharpener
42p

ruler
55p

You have £10·00 to spend in the shop. Write how many of each item you could buy:

1. scissors
2. notebook
3. pencil sharpener
4. pen
5. rubber
6. pencil case
7. ruler

The shop puts on a special offer.

You can buy any three items for £1·16.

Will the special offer save you money if you buy three:

Special offer!
Any three items
£1·16

8. rulers?
9. notebooks?
10. rubbers?
11. pencil sharpeners?
12. pens?

Will the special offer save you money on each set?

13. a ruler, a pen and a rubber
14. a rubber, a pencil sharpener and a ruler
15. a notebook, a pencil sharpener and a rubber
16. a rubber, a pencil sharpener and a pen

The shop offers a 10% discount if you buy five or more items. How much will you save if you buy two of each item?

Percentages and fractions

What percentage of each shape is shaded? What percentage is not shaded?

1.   2.   3.   4.   5.

Remember:

One whole = 100%

$\frac{1}{2}$ = 50%

$\frac{1}{4}$ = 25%

$\frac{1}{10}$ = 10%

6.   7.   8.

Write each amount.

9.   10% of £3·00   10.   10% of £7·00

11.   50% of £1·00   12.   50% of £5·00

13.   25% of £5·00   14.   25% of £4·00

Write what must be added to each number to make 5.

1. $1\frac{3}{5}$ 2. $3\frac{7}{10}$ 3. $4\frac{3}{9}$

4. $3\frac{4}{8}$ 5. $1\frac{2}{3}$ 6. $2\frac{7}{8}$

Write the odd one out in each set.

7.    8.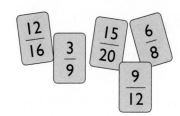

9.    10.

Write some equivalent fractions for the odd one out in each set.

5

Spectacular sweets

These are the prices at the Spectacular Sweet Shop:

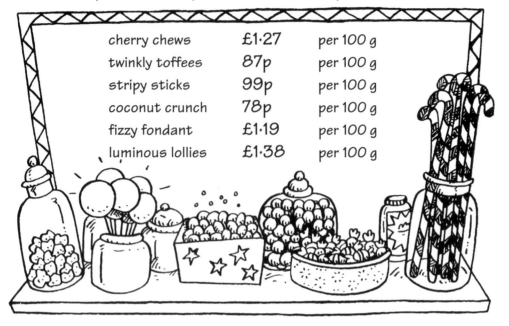

cherry chews	£1·27	per 100 g
twinkly toffees	87p	per 100 g
stripy sticks	99p	per 100 g
coconut crunch	78p	per 100 g
fizzy fondant	£1·19	per 100 g
luminous lollies	£1·38	per 100 g

Estimate first, then use your calculator to add up each bill.

1.
100 g fizzy fondant
200 g stripy sticks
100 g coconut crunch

2.
100 g stripy sticks
100 g cherry chews
200 g twinkly toffees

3.
100 g fizzy fondant
200 g stripy sticks
300 g luminous lollies

4.
200 g coconut crunch
100 g cherry chews
150 g luminous lollies

5.
100 g twinkly toffees
100 g stripy sticks
200 g cherry chews
150 g luminous lollies

6.
200 g fizzy fondant
100 g cherry chews
150 g coconut crunch
200 g twinkly toffees

What would the total bill be to buy $\frac{1}{2}$ kg of each type of sweet?

Island hopping

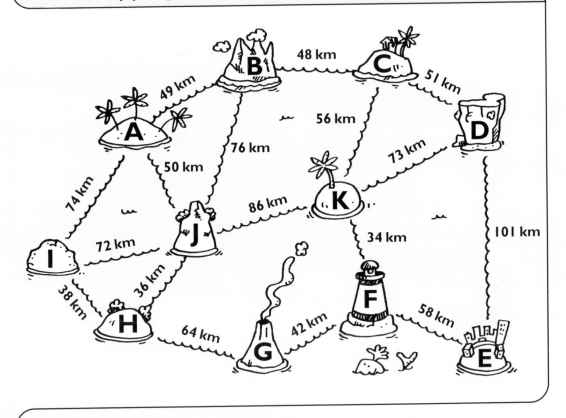

Work out the shortest route between each pair of islands:

1. A and K
2. C and I
3. D and G
4. F and A
5. G and B
6. D and I

The island ferry cannot travel further than 70 km without stopping for fuel. Work out the shortest route it can take between each pair of islands:

7. I and B
8. E and A
9. G and B
10. D and H
11. A and F
12. H and C

A traveller has a ferry pass to travel up to 500 km. Which islands could she visit if she must start and finish at the airport on island E?

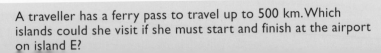

Angles

Write whether each angle is acute, obtuse, or a right angle and estimate its size.

1.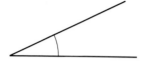

2.

3.

4.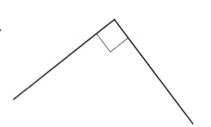

5.

6.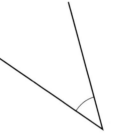

7.

8.

Now use a protractor to measure each angle.

Draw these angles:

1. 70°   **2.** 140°

3. 90°   **4.** 30°

5. 165°   **6.** 180°

Draw some regular and irregular polygons. Measure all the internal angles. Count the number of sides. What do you notice?

Number wall

Take one number from each cloud and an operator from the sun. Can you make a multiple of 2? A multiple of 3? A multiple of 4? A multiple of 5? And a multiple of 10?

Find routes up the wall following multiples of 7 or 9. You can move up or across but not down. Record your routes as lists.

1830	1773	707	487	513	1253
927	1042	1610	819	875	
736	378	805	243	892	742
245	1071	162	882	280	
18	791	210	695	252	351
1042	84	947	365	279	
22	106	56	46	221	486
364	14	49	27	54	

⑦ ⑦ ⑦ ⑨ ⑨

Draw your own number wall for multiples of 8. Swap with a friend. Can you find a route through their wall?

9

Problems

1. A bucket can hold 16 litres of water. If it is a quarter full, how much water is in it?
   If it is filled up to three quarters full, how much more water has been put in it?

2. If 200 grams of sugar cost 45p, how much would 1 kilogram cost?

3. Jamie is 1 metre 26 centimetres tall. He is 16 centimetres taller than Ali who is 20 centimetres taller than Sasha. How tall is Ali? How tall is Sasha?

Write the total length of each set of ribbons in metres.

4.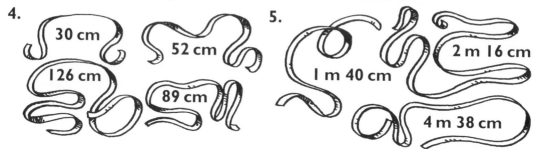

   30 cm   52 cm

   126 cm   89 cm

5. 2 m 16 cm

   1 m 40 cm

   4 m 38 cm

6. A recipe needs 75 g of butter, 275 g of flour, 125 g of sugar. What is the total weight of the ingredients?

7. The recipe is doubled. What is the total weight now?

8. There are 50 litres of orange juice for sports day. If a cup holds 250 millilitres, how many cups can be filled with orange juice?

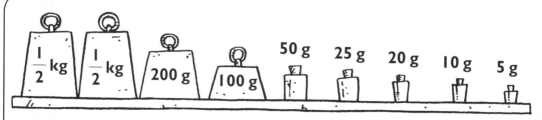

$\frac{1}{2}$ kg $\frac{1}{2}$ kg   200 g   100 g   50 g   25 g   20 g   10 g   5 g

Which weights would you use to make each total?

1. 380 g
2. 0·6 kg
3. 830 g
4. 0·57 kg
5. 335 g
6. 695 g
7. 0·405 kg
8. 0·05 kg
9. 0·79 kg

How could you divide the weights into two equal groups?

Timetables

Quackbridge	7:22	8:32	9:12	9:37	10:12
Barking	7:27	8:37	–	9:42	–
Crowville	7:32	8:42	–	9:47	–
Neighwick	7:38	8:48	–	9:53	–
Little Bleatings	7:48	8:58	–	10:03	–
Mooford	7:53	9:03	9:29	10:08	10:33
Upper Tweeting	7:55	9:06	–	10:12	–
Cluckton	8:00	9:11	–	10:17	–
Baahampton	8:04	9:15	–	10:21	–
Mewbury	8:08	9:19	9:47	10:24	10:44

1. What time does the 10:12 from Quackbridge arrive at Mewbury?

2. How long does it take to get there?

3. If you catch the 9:03 from Mooford, what time do you arrive at Baahampton?

4. You walk to Mooford station and get there at 10:05. How long must you wait for the next train?

5. You walk to Upper Tweeting station and arrive there at 9:20. If you catch the next train, what time will you arrive in Mewbury?

6. Which train takes the least time to travel from Quackbridge to Mewbury? How long does it take?

7. Which train takes the most time to travel from Little Bleatings to Upper Tweeting? How much longer does it take than the fastest train?

8. The 9:12 from Quackbridge is delayed by 20 minutes. What time does it reach Mewbury?

Write a timetable for a train leaving Mewbury at 17:21, which stops at every station to Quackbridge if the times between stations are the same as the 8:32 from Quackbridge.

Perimeters

How much fencing is needed to go round each field?

1.
75·2 m
16 m

2.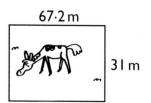
67·2 m
31 m

3.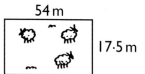
54 m
17·5 m

4.
97·6 m
24·3 m

5.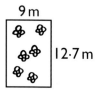
9 m
12·7 m

6.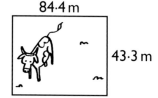
84·4 m
43·3 m

7.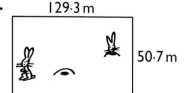
129·3 m
50·7 m

8.
99·9 m
9 m

Write the perimeter of each shape:

9. a square with sides measuring 5·6 cm

10. a rectangle with sides measuring 2 cm and 3·7 cm

11. a rectangle with sides measuring 5·7 cm and 2·4 cm

12. a square with sides measuring 9·6 cm

13. a rectangle with sides measuring 2·1 cm and 11·3 cm

14. a rectangle with sides measuring 1·9 cm and 8·2 cm

Use a calculator to find the area of each field and shape.

Exchange rates

These are the exchange rates at the bank. They show how much of each currency you get for £1·00.

KES 115   **Kenyan Shillings**

HK $11   **Hong Kong Dollars**

$1·5   **U.S. Dollars**

NZ $3·5   **New Zealand Dollars**

40 RUB   **Russian Roubles**

Use a calculator to help you answer each question.

Write how many Hong Kong Dollars you get for each amount:

1. £10·00

2. £12·00

3. £18·00

4. £150·00

Write how many Kenyan Shillings you get for each amount:

5. £5·00

6. £15·00

7. £32·00

8. £50·00

9. You have 75 U.S. Dollars. How much did they cost in pounds?

10. How much would it cost to buy 3025 Hong Kong Dollars?

11. How many New Zealand Dollars would you get for £200·00?

12. How much of each currency would you get for £75·00?

How many Russian Roubles would you get for 484 Hong Kong Dollars?

13

Skyscraper

The super skyscraper on Planet Zax has 21 floors above the ground. It has another 20 floors below the ground!

The ground floor is Floor 0.

Zag gets in the lift and records where each trip takes her. She adds the number of floors she goes up, and subtracts the number of floors she goes down.

She always starts at Floor 0.

Write the calculations to work out where she ends up each time.

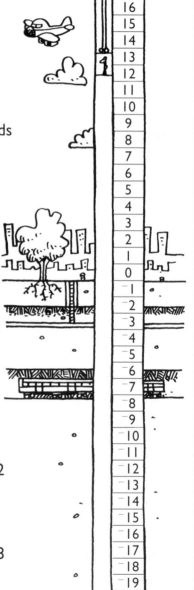

Example

Down 3, up 2, up 4, down 5

$0 - 3 + 2 + 4 - 5 = {}^-2$ Floor $^-2$

1. Down 5, up 11, down 6, up 12, down 20, up 15
2. Down 16, up 12, down 3, up 10, down 23
3. Down 12, up 6, down 15, up 24, down 20
4. Down 1, up 18, down 30, up 4
5. Down 3, up 15, down 18, up 25
6. Down 7, down 4, down 6, up 8, up 2, down 12
7. Down 5, up 16, up 4, down 17, down 3
8. Up 12, down 13, down 6, up 7, down 8
9. Down 5, down 6, up 11, down 9, down 3, up 8
10. Down 7, down 4, up 8, up 9, down 7, down 2

If it takes 20 seconds to travel between floors, how long does it take to travel from Floor 8 to Floor $^-$13?

Space factors

Any satellite whose number matches a statement can go into orbit.

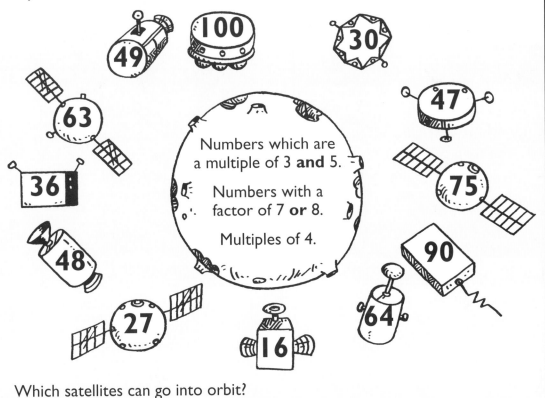

Numbers which are a multiple of 3 **and** 5.

Numbers with a factor of 7 **or** 8.

Multiples of 4.

Which satellites can go into orbit?

Divide each star number by each rocket number. Show your working.

Write the remainder if there is one.

Write all the factors of each satellite and star number.

Problems

1. Jane buys a CD player for £78·00 and a CD for £15·00. How much does she have left from £100·00?

2. Ice creams cost 78p each. How much do 9 ice creams cost?

3. Hardeep buys a rug for £12·89, a jug for £3·59 and a mug for £1·99. How much change does he have from £20·00?

4. If a slice of pizza costs £2·15 and a glass of lemonade costs £1·15, how much does it cost to buy three slices of pizza and three glasses of lemonade?

5. Giles saves £1·25 a week. How long will it take him to save £100·00?

6. Susie saves £12·50 a month. How long will it take her to save £200·00?

7. Dominic saves 83p a week. How long will it take him to save £60·00?

8. Natalie buys four books. Two of them cost £7·99 each, one costs £5·50 and the other costs £3·65. How much does she spend?

9. Marcus spends £30·00 in a bookshop. He buys five books. Two of the books cost £4·67 each, one cost £8·19 and one cost £4·72. How much did the other book cost?

Percentages

What percentage of each jumper is wool?

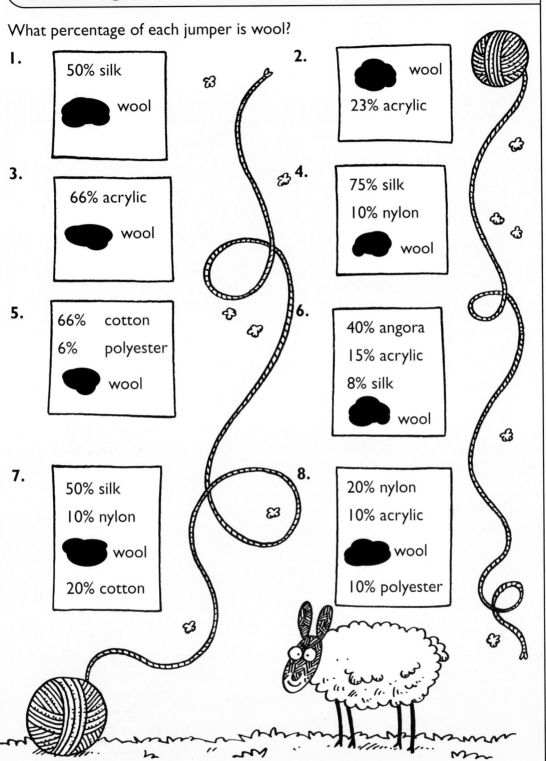

1.
50% silk

wool

2.
wool

23% acrylic

3.
66% acrylic

wool

4.
75% silk

10% nylon

wool

5.
66%   cotton

6%   polyester

wool

6.
40% angora

15% acrylic

8% silk

wool

7.
50% silk

10% nylon

wool

20% cotton

8.
20% nylon

10% acrylic

wool

10% polyester

Wool, cotton, angora and silk are natural fibres. Acrylic, nylon and polyester are man-made fibres. Write the percentage of natural and man-made fibres in each jumper

Purse percentages

How much does each person spend?

1.
   50% of £100·00

2.
   50% of £75·00

3.
   10% of £15·00

4.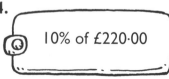
   10% of £220·00

5.
   25% of £40·00

6.
   75% of £16·00

7.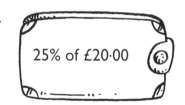
   25% of £20·00

8.
   75% of £60·00

9.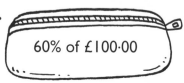
   60% of £100·00

10.
    40% of £200·00

11.
    20% of £20·00

12.
    30% of £50·00

13. What percentage of their money does each person have left?

14. How much money do they each have left?

Each person loses 20% of the money they have left in their purse. Write how much each has now.

Moving shapes

Write whether each shape is a reflection, a rotation, or a translation of the shaded shape.

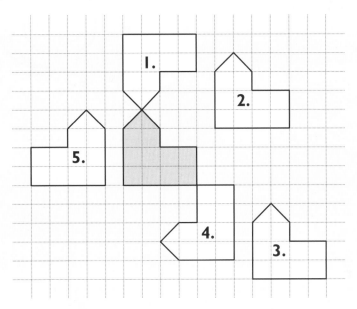

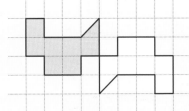
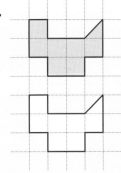
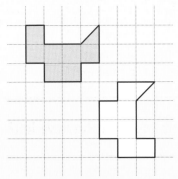
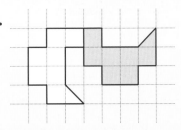

6.

7.

8.

9.

Copy the shaded shapes onto graph paper.
Draw 90° clockwise rotations of the shapes
about each of their corners.

Coordinates

Write the coordinates of each point.

Example

a $(^-4, 4)$

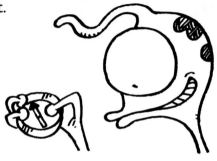

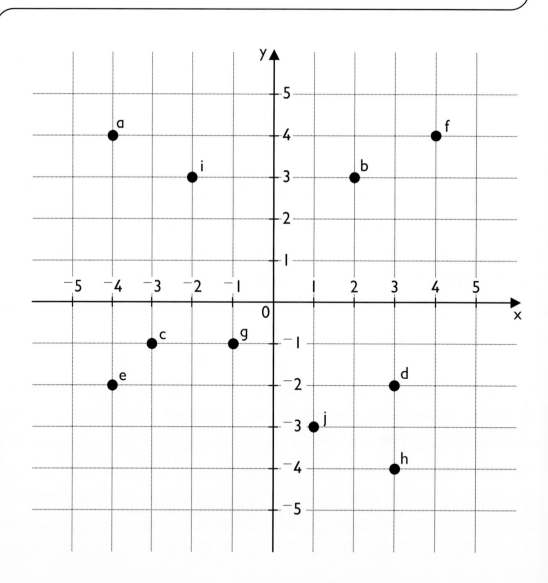

Write the coordinates of each of the points after a reflection in the x-axis, then the y-axis.

CD time

The length of each track on a CD is listed in minutes and seconds.

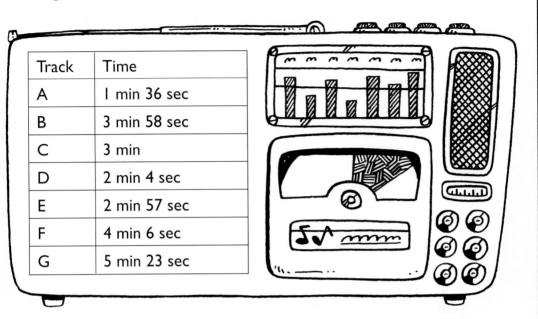

Track	Time
A	1 min 36 sec
B	3 min 58 sec
C	3 min
D	2 min 4 sec
E	2 min 57 sec
F	4 min 6 sec
G	5 min 23 sec

Write how long it would take to play these tracks:

1. C and F

2. A and D

3. B and E

4. A and G

5. A, C and F

6. D, E and G

7. B, C and E

8. B, D and F.

Write a combination of tracks you could play in each time. Try to have as little time left over as possible.

9. 5 minutes

10. 7 minutes

11. $7\frac{1}{2}$ minutes

12. 8 minutes

13. 10 minutes

14. 12 minutes

The whole CD plays on repeat three times. How long does it play in total?

Length

Write each distance in kilometres.

1.
4638 m

2.
6512 m

3.
1410 m

4.
4250 m

Write each distance in metres.

5.
5·5 km

6.
7·2 km

7.
0·75 km

8.
$4\frac{3}{4}$ km

Write each length in metres.

9. 4010 cm   **10.** 3904 cm   **11.** 20 500 cm   **12.** 10 003 cm

Write each length in centimetres.

13. 2·7 metres   **14.** 0·14 metres   **15.** $2\frac{3}{10}$ metres   **16.** $1\frac{2}{5}$ metres

17. Marcie cycles to school and back every day from Monday to Friday. Her school is 1·25 km from her home. How far does she cycle in a week?

18. Jenny is 15 cm shorter than Jacob. Shabita is 10 cm taller than Jenny. How much taller is Jacob than Shabita?

19. Fluffy the kitten was 12 cm long when he was born. He is now 10 weeks old and 30 cm long. He grew the same amount each week. How much did he grow each week?

20. Sarah bought a plant that was 20 cm tall. Each week, it doubled in height. How tall was it after five weeks?

Pool data

Information was collected at the local swimming pool one Saturday.

1. Draw a pictogram to show this information. Use one symbol to represent 4 swimmers

Favourite swimming strokes

Stroke	Number of swimmers
Crawl	17
Breaststroke	15
Backstroke	19
Butterfly	9

2. Draw a line graph to show this information.

Time	Temperature of pool water
09:00	23°
10:00	24°
11:00	26°
12:00	25°
13:00	27°
14:00	26°

3. Draw a bar graph to show this information.

Ages of 60 swimmers

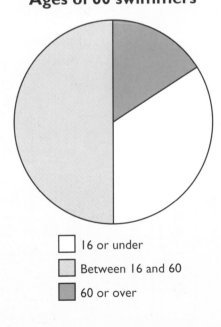

☐ 16 or under
◻ Between 16 and 60
◼ 60 or over

4. Draw a pie chart to show this information.

Number of swimmers using equipment

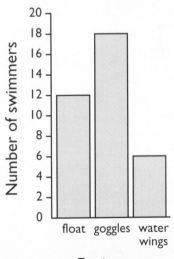

Equipment

Collect some information of your own. Draw different types of graph to display your data.

Mode, mean and median

The mode is the value which occurs most often.

The median is the middle value in a set of data. You must put the values in order before you can find the median.

The mean is an average you find by adding together all the values and dividing the total by the number of values.

Here are the marks at a skating competition:

7   4   7   7   8   4   5

1. What is the mode score?

    What is the median score?

    What is the mean score?

Find the mode, mean and median of each set of scores.

2. 2 5 2 4 7

3. 6 7 8 7 2

4. 2 3 2 1 2

5. 2 9 3 6 5

    9 1

 Write what the averages tell you about the skaters in each competition.

Mode, mean, median and range

Each member of Class 5 and Class 6 has twenty turns at shooting into the basketball net. They each record the number of baskets they score.

1. Use a calculator to help you find the mode, mean and median score for each class.

Class 5

13   15   17   14   15   16   19   14   20   15   18   16   17   15   16

Class 6

12   15   13   11   16   15   17   18   16   14   16   20   16   14   12

The range of a set of data is the difference between the largest and the smallest value.

2. What is the range of each set of scores?

3. Work out the range of each set of scores on page 24.

 Roll a dice five times. Count how many times you roll a 6. Repeat ten times, then find the mode, mean, median and range for the number of 6s rolled.

Mode, mean and median

1. Jodie, Niall and Bruce go bowling. They each have seven turns. Work out each child's mode, median and mean score.

2. What is the mode, median and mean of all the scores together?

Jodie	6	5	3	5	5	8	3
Niall	1	10	9	3	8	9	9
Bruce	5	3	2	4	3	1	3

The football team needs a new goalkeeper. There are three goalkeepers to choose from.

The table shows how many goals they each saved in the last three seasons.

	Season 1	Season 2	Season 3
Goalkeeper A	25	23	18
Goalkeeper B	27	28	29
Goalkeeper C	15	25	23

3. Work out the mean number of goals each goalkeeper saves per season.

4. Which goalkeeper would you choose? Why?

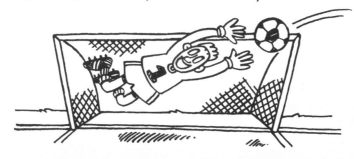

Another goalkeeper saved 31 goals last season and 27 the season before. Is this goalkeeper better than the one you chose?

Planet puzzle

Copy the asteroid numbers into three sets of three so that each set adds to the same total.

Each planet total is made by adding three of the star numbers together and subtracting the fourth. Which star number in each set was subtracted?

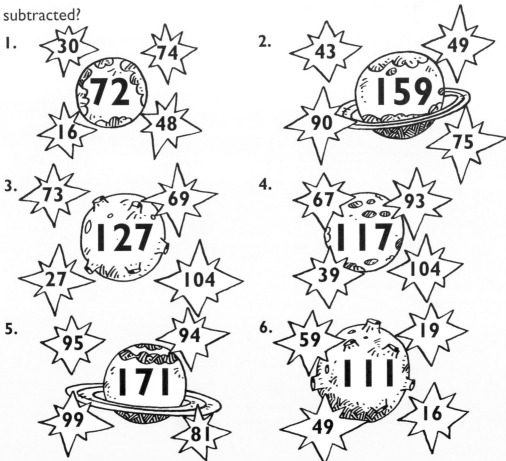

1. 30 74 72 16 48

2. 43 49 159 90 75

3. 73 69 127 27 104

4. 67 93 117 39 104

5. 95 94 171 99 81

6. 59 19 111 49 16

Puzzling problems

Each letter stands for a digit. No digit matches more than one letter.

What digit does each letter stand for? There is more than one correct answer!

```
    S U N
+ S A N D
---------
B E A C H
```

Remove the picture cards and aces from a pack of playing cards.

Now try to arrange the cards you have left in 6 rows and 6 columns so that all of these statements are true:

the total of each row is 36

the total of each column is 36

each row includes three red cards and three black

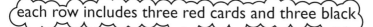

each column includes three red cards and three black

the red and black cards are arranged in a 'checkerboard' pattern

Multiplication

Multiply each 3-digit number by 9.

Reverse the digits in your answer and add it to the first answer.

Now add together the digits in your total.

What do you find?

Example

$154 \times 9 = 1386$

Reverse digits $\rightarrow 6831$.

$1386 + 6831 = 8217$

$8 + 2 + 1 + 7 = 18$

154   163   953   236

527   381   176   451

Write as many pairs of factors for each number as you can.

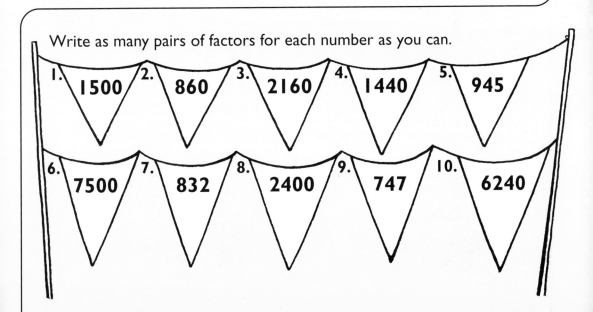

1. 1500   2. 860   3. 2160   4. 1440   5. 945

6. 7500   7. 832   8. 2400   9. 747   10. 6240

 Multiply each of the flag numbers by 3, 5, 7 and 9.

Museum shop 1

There is a sale at the museum shop. Each price is reduced by 25%.

badge £1·60
poster £3·60
sweatshirt £16·00
guide book £3·00
key ring £4·40
jigsaw £4·00
video £12·00
rucksack £6·00
T-shirt £5·80
mobile £18·00
cuddly toy £7·20

1. What will each item cost now? List the new prices.
2. How much will two videos cost now?
3. How much will three sweatshirts cost now?
4. How much will it cost now to buy a key ring and a poster?
5. How much will it cost now to buy a badge and a rucksack?
6. How much cheaper than before the sale is a jigsaw now?
7. How much cheaper than before the sale is a mobile now?
8. How much cheaper than before the sale is it to buy a mobile and a sweatshirt?
9. What could I buy for £20·00 at the new prices?
10. What three items could I now buy for £10·00?

On double discount day the prices are reduced by 50%. Find the answers to the questions above on this day.

Museum shop 2

The sale has now finished and everything in the museum shop is being sold at the original prices on page 30.

Work out how much each person has spent and how much change they will get from £20·00.

1. Katie buys a video, a rucksack and a badge.

2. Amit buys a guide book, a jigsaw and a poster.

3. Molly buys a mobile and a badge.

4. Jay buys a T-shirt, two badges, a guide book and a poster.

5. Ollie buys two posters, a cuddly toy and a key ring.

6. Rana buys a sweatshirt and two badges.

Find a combination which costs exactly:

7. £9·20

8. £14·20

9. £10·20

10. £19·20

11. £12·40

12. £14·60

 Mrs Evans buys each of her three children two presents each from the museum shop. She spends £32·40 in total. What does she buy her children?

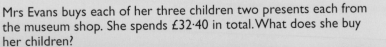

Ratio and proportion

1. There are three times as many bananas as oranges in Joel's fruit bowl. He has six bananas. How many oranges does he have?

2. For a recipe you must use 50 g of butter for every 25 g of sugar. Write how much butter you need for each amount of sugar:

   a 50 g

   b 250 g

   c 75 g

   d 100 g

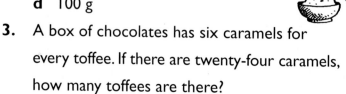

3. A box of chocolates has six caramels for every toffee. If there are twenty-four caramels, how many toffees are there?

4. Matt is reading a recipe. He needs $\frac{1}{2}$ teaspoon of baking powder for every 500 g of flour. How much baking powder does he need if he has $1\frac{1}{2}$ kg of flour?

5. For every rabbit in pets' corner there are two guinea pigs. There are nine animals altogether. How many of them are guinea pigs?

6. In term time, Jen goes to school on five days of each week and stays at home for two days. For every five days at school, she is at home for two. How many days will she be at home in four weeks?

7. For every six pairs of blue socks in her drawer, Katya has five pairs of red socks. She has twelve pairs of blue socks. How many pairs of red socks does she have?

Alien visit

250 aliens visited Earth. Here are some facts about what they did while they were here:

50% used buses

28% liked ice cream

60% went to the cinema

30% bought trainers

80% bought chocolate

90% went to the beach

1. What percentage did not use buses?
2. How many aliens did not use buses?
3. What percentage did not like ice cream?
4. How many did not like ice cream?
5. How many aliens went to the cinema?
6. What percentage did not go to the cinema?
7. What percentage did not buy trainers?
8. How many aliens bought trainers?
9. How many aliens bought chocolate?
10. How many aliens did not go to the beach?

Work out:

11. 25% of £25·00
12. 75% of £4·00
13. 50% of £50·00
14. 10% of £30·00
15. $\frac{1}{4}$ of £1000·00
16. 10% of £5·00
17. 50% of £1800·00
18. 90% of £1000·00
19. 0·5 of £280·00
20. 90% of £100·00
21. $\frac{1}{2}$ of £90·00
22. $\frac{1}{4}$ of £180·00
23. 25% of £560·00
24. 20% of £420·00

Which questions have the same answers?

Find 15% of the amounts above.

Probability

Write your answers as fractions.

For example, a one in six chance is written as $\frac{1}{6}$.

You throw a 6-sided dice.

1. What is the probability of throwing an even number?
2. What is the probability of throwing an odd number?
3. What is the probability of throwing a 6?
4. What is the probability of throwing a 2?
5. What is the probability of throwing a 4 or a 5?
6. What is the probability of throwing a multiple of 3?

You pick a card from a full pack.

Write the probability that your card is:

7. a red card
8. a black card
9. a heart
10. a spade
11. a two
12. an even number
13. a king
14. the seven of diamonds
15. a picture card
16. the ace of clubs

52 cards in a pack

13 cards in each suit

What are the probabilities of these events if the picture cards are removed from the pack?

Mean and range

Use a calculator to find the mean and the range of each set of prices.

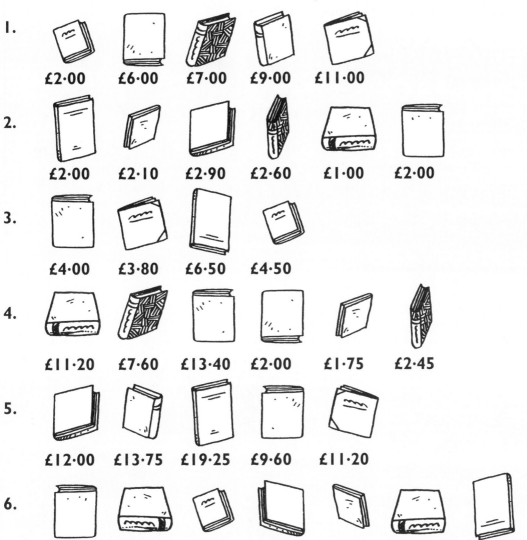

1. £2·00   £6·00   £7·00   £9·00   £11·00

2. £2·00   £2·10   £2·90   £2·60   £1·00   £2·00

3. £4·00   £3·80   £6·50   £4·50

4. £11·20   £7·60   £13·40   £2·00   £1·75   £2·45

5. £12·00   £13·75   £19·25   £9·60   £11·20

6. £2·80   £3·65   £4·35   £12·20   £2·40   £6·50   £1·70

Write down the names of everybody in your group. Count the number of letters in each name. What is the mean number of letters in a name? What is the range of the number of letters?

Find the mode and median number of letters in the names that you write down.

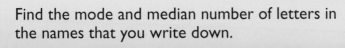

Dog data

The height, weight and age of each dog at a dog show is recorded in a table.

Height (cm)	49	52	66	31	45	51	28
Weight (kg)	25	30	38	8	12	13	7
Age (years)	3	4	6	10	5	8	6

Find each fact about the dogs:

1. median weight
2. mean weight
3. median age
4. mean age
5. median height
6. mean height
7. range of heights
8. range of weights
9. range of ages

Another dog which is 54 cm high and weighs 51 kg enters the dog show. How do the mean heights and weights change?

Angles

Write whether each angle is acute, obtuse or a right angle, and estimate its size.

1.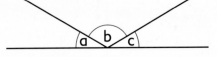

2.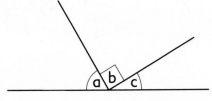

3.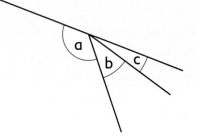

4.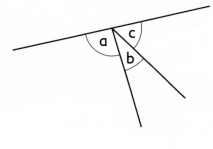

Now use a protractor to measure each angle. How close were your estimates?

Use a protractor to measure each angle.

Add together the angles in each triangle.

What do you notice?

5.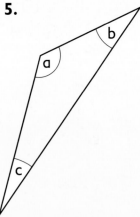

6.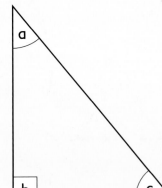

7.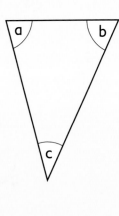

Tessellations

Which shapes would tessellate?

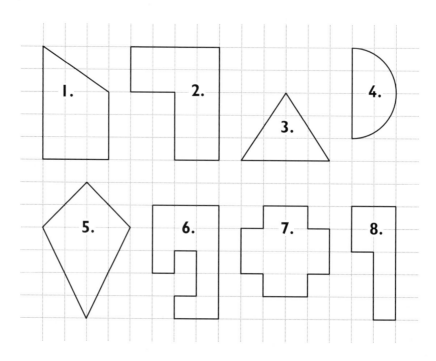

1.
2.
3.
4.
5.
6.
7.
8.

Draw the tessellations on squared paper.

Investigate tessellation using capital letters. Try these first:

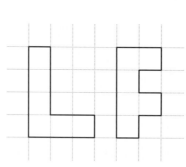

Now try other letters.

Draw your patterns on squared paper.

Money bags

3·6 grams   7·1 grams

Write the weight of:

1. 100 1p coins
2. 150 2p coins
3. 50 2p coins
4. 20 1p coins and 100 2p coins

Instead of counting each coin in big bags of coins, people in banks weigh the bags to work out how many coins there are.

Write how many 1p coins there are in each bag:

5.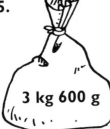
3 kg 600 g

6.
1800 g

7.
900 g

8.
18 kg

Write how many 2p coins there are in each bag:

9.
710 g

10.
7.1 kg

11.
1 kg 775 g

12.
355 g

13. There are five coins in the bag. It weighs 25 g. How many of the coins are 2p coins and how many are 1p coins?

   Try estimating possible combinations first.

A 5p coin weighs 3.25 g. A bag of 1p and 5p coins weighs 31 g. How many 1p coins and how many 5p coins are there?

Teleport

Aliens on Planet Zax travel by teleport.
However, if they take more than
4 kg 200 g of luggage, it won't work.

What fraction of their luggage must
each alien leave behind?

1.
8 kg 400 g

2.
12 kg 600 g

3.
6 kg 300 g

4.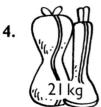
21 kg

5.
25 kg 200 g

How many ways of sharing this luggage could three aliens find so that they can take it all?

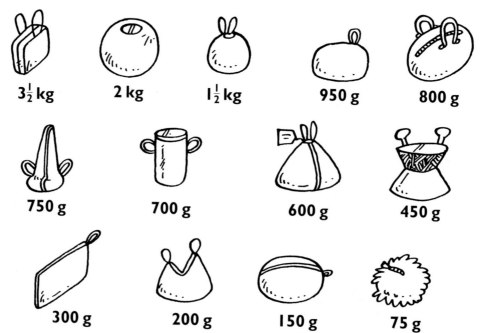

$3\frac{1}{2}$ kg   2 kg $1\frac{1}{2}$ kg   950 g   800 g

750 g   700 g   600 g   450 g

300 g   200 g   150 g   75 g

  How many ways could four aliens share the luggage to take it in a teleport with a luggage weight limit of 3 kg 600 g?

Time problems

Write each time as a 24-hour clock time:

1. quarter to seven in the morning
2. 9 o'clock in the evening
3. twenty-five past two in the afternoon
4. 1:00 p.m.

What time does each flight leave?

Write each time as a digital 12-hour clock time.

5. 19:00

6. 11:50

7. 13:45

8. 09:15

9. 17:30

10. 15:05

Work out the shortest travelling time between each pair of places:

11. B and I
12. J and A
13. H and B

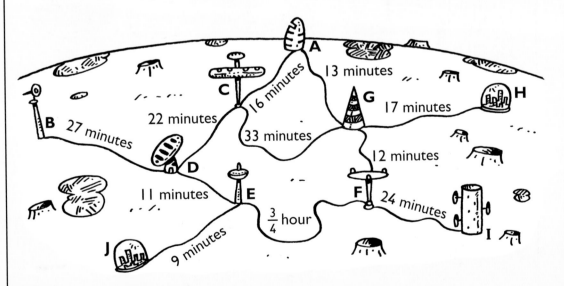

A space buggy driver takes 1 hour 28 minutes to travel from H to J. Which route does he take?

Plane problems

These are the time differences between London and other cities around the world.

New York	Paris	Tokyo	Sydney
⁻5 hours	+1 hour	+9 hours	+10 hours

The travel agent has spilt coffee all over the information sheet! Use the time differences to work out the missing information for each flight.

	Flight	Departure (local time)	Arrival (local time)	Length of flight
1.	London to Paris	11:00		1 hour
2.	New York to London	09:30		7 hours
3.	Paris to New York		20:30	8 hours 35 minutes
4.	London to Tokyo	14:10	11:00 (the next day)	
5.	Sydney to London		06:40 (the next day)	23 hours 35 minutes
6.	Tokyo to Paris	11:05	15:20	
7.	New York to Tokyo	09:41	15:10 (the next day)	
8.	New York to Sydney	08:00		22 hours 25 minutes

Area and perimeter

Write the perimeter of each shape.

1.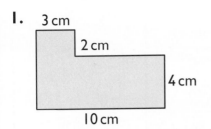
3 cm
2 cm
4 cm
10 cm

2.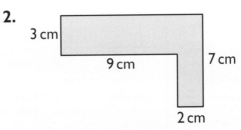
3 cm
9 cm
7 cm
2 cm

3.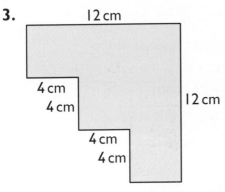
12 cm
4 cm
4 cm
12 cm
4 cm
4 cm

4.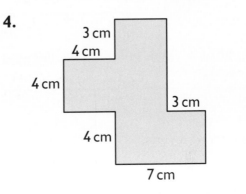
3 cm
4 cm
4 cm
3 cm
4 cm
7 cm

Now can you calculate the area of each shape?

Work out the width of each rectangle.

5.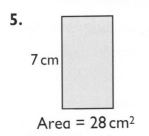
7 cm
Area = 28 cm²

6.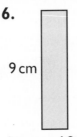
9 cm
Area = 18 cm²

7.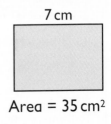
7 cm
Area = 35 cm²

8.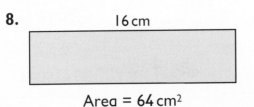
16 cm
Area = 64 cm²

9.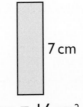
7 cm
Area = 14 cm²

10.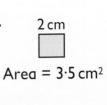
2 cm
Area = 3·5 cm²

Work out the measurements of four different
quadrilaterals with a perimeter of 16 cm.

Travel

The chart shows the cost of travelling to two seaside towns.

	Suncliff	Sandbury
Train	£42·80	£32·20
Coach	£20·00	£16·40
Plane	£60·60	£40·96

If you book a week before travelling you only pay 75% of each price.

1. Work out how much cheaper each ticket is if it is bought a week before travelling.

Which is cheaper and by how much?

2.   **a** a plane ticket to Suncliff bought a week before
  or
    b a plane ticket to Sandbury bought on the day

3.   **a** a train ticket to Suncliff bought a week before
  or
    b a train ticket to Sandbury bought on the day

4.   **a** two plane tickets to Suncliff bought on the day
  or
    b three plane tickets to Sandbury bought on the day

5.   **a** three coach tickets to Suncliff bought a week before
  or
    b two train tickets to Sandbury bought a week before

Where is each group going and how are they travelling?

6. Three people buy tickets on the day they travel. They spend £49·20.
7. Five people buy tickets on the day they travel. They spend £214·00.
8. Two people buy tickets a week before they travel. They spend £61·44.
9. Four people buy tickets a week before they travel. They spend £60·00.

Money problems

Mrs Simkins and Mrs Wilkins go on holiday.
Mrs Simkins pays £497 to stay at the
Sea View hotel for 7 days.
Mrs Wilkins pays £350 to stay at the
Sandy Bay hotel for 5 days.

1.   Which hotel is better value?

2.   What is the price per day at each hotel?

Five rugby balls and a football cost £55.

Five footballs and a rugby ball cost £35.

3.   How much does a football cost?

4.   How much does a rugby ball cost?

Two tennis balls and two golf balls cost £7·00.

Three golf balls and one tennis ball cost £7·50.

5.   How much does a tennis ball cost?

6.   How much does a golf ball cost?

Try to find each amount without a calculator:

7.   50% of £2350·40

8.   30% of £850·00

9.   70% of £600·00

10.   80% of 200 kg

11.   15% of 60 litres

12.   90% of £8000·00

Find 35% of each amount or quantity.

Challenge

Add two numbers and subtract another from your total. Try to make:

1. 373
2. 168
3. a total divisible by 3
4. a total divisible by 4

Use a sign and a number from the centre of the sunflower with a number from a petal to make a total.

Can you make the same total in more than one way?

£750·00   £98·00

£2200·00

+   −   £216·15

£28·50   ×   ÷

£86·75

£333·00

£67·00

9   8   3   4   7   2   10   12   5